Cynnwys

Cyflwyniad/Introduction

Cyflwyniad

Cyfres o naw o lyfrau darllen ffeithiol ar gyfer disgyblion CA2 sy'n dysgu'r Gymraeg fel ail iaith yw **Cyfres y Gwdihŵ**. Ceir tair thema yn y gyfres, sef Hamdden, Anifeiliaid a Theithio.

Mae'r gyfres wedi ei bwriadu ar gyfer dysgwyr sy'n gweithio ar lefelau 2-4. Ceir un llyfr ar bob thema ar bob lefel.

Lliw cefndir y logo sy'n dangos lefel pob llyfr. Dyma'r lliwiau:
> Oren ar gyfer Lefel 2
> Gwyrdd ar gyfer Lefel 3
> Glas ar gyfer Lefel 4.

Mae'r Llawlyfr hwn yn cyd-fynd â'r tri llyfr ar Hamdden, sef **Byd y Bêl** (lefel 2), **Hwyl y Gwersyll** (lefel 3) a **Llethrau Llithrig!** (lefel 4).

Ceir cyfieithiad Saesneg o destun pob un o'r llyfrau ar ddechrau adran y llyfr hwnnw. Yn dilyn hynny, ceir awgrymiadau ynglŷn â chyflwyno'r llyfr a gweithgareddau posibl yn seiliedig ar y cynnwys.

Introduction

Cyfres y Gwdihŵ is a series of nine factual reading books for KS2 pupils who are learning Welsh as a second language. There are three themes in the series, namely Leisure, Animals and Travelling.

The series is intended for learners working on levels 2-4. There is one book on each theme on each level.

The level of each book is shown by the colour of the logo's background. These are the colours:
> Orange for Level 2
> Green for Level 3
> Blue for Level 4.

This Handbook accompanies the three books on Leisure, namely **Byd y Bêl** (level 2), **Hwyl y Gwersyll** (level 3) and **Llethrau Llithrig!** (level 4).

There is an English translation of the text of each book at the beginning of the section on that book. This is followed by suggestions on how to present the book and for possible activities based on the content.

Byd y Bêl

page 4 — Cricket

What do you need to play cricket?

a shirt   gloves   a pair of trousers
a bat   a ball   a helmet   pads

This is the Glamorgan cricket team.
There are eleven players in the team.

page 5 — Cricket

When playing cricket you have to...

bowl
              run   bat
jump
              throw the ball   catch the ball

the boundary
wicket-keeper   *batsman*
the wicket   *bowler*
              A cricket pitch

The batsman wears a helmet, pads and gloves.
The bowler throws the ball very quickly.
The batsman bats the ball and then runs from one wicket to the other to score a run.

page 6 — Tennis

What do you need to play tennis?

a pair of shorts   a shirt
or   a racket
a skirt   trainers
                                 a ball

              Two or four can play tennis.

Tennis — page 7

When playing tennis you have to...

hit the ball   bounce the ball
              throw the ball   stretch
run

net   *line*

              A tennis court

The players hit the ball back and forth over the net.

Rugby — page 8

What do you need to play rugby?

socks   a pair of shorts   a shirt
boots   *Go to the sin bin!*
a ball   a referee

This is the Welsh rugby team. They are wearing the red shirts of Wales. There are fifteen players in the team.

Rugby — page 9

When playing rugby you have to...

                    kick   throw the ball
pass   catch the ball
scrum   tackle   score a try

How many points?
try – five   conversion – two   drop-goal – three

the posts   *the field*
                                           the try line

The Millenium Stadium. The Welsh rugby team play here.

page 10 ———————————————— Snooker

This is the snooker table at the beginning of the game.

a pocket

How many points?
red – one   yellow – two   green – three
brown – four   blue – five   pink – six
black – seven

What do you need to play snooker?
a triangle   chalk   a cue

page 11 ———————————————— Snooker

When playing snooker you have to...

place the balls   hit the ball   aim the cue

stretch

pot the ball

Here are the famous players, Mark Williams and Matthew Stevens.
Mark comes from the village of Cwm, in Blaenau Gwent.
Matthew comes from Llangynnwr, near Carmarthen.

page 12 ———————————————— Netball

What do you need to play netball?

a skirt   trainers
          a shirt
    a ball   a tabard

This is the Welsh netball team.
There are seven players in the team.
Every one of the Welsh players is wearing a red tabard.

Netball ———————————————— page 13

When playing netball you have to...
                              throw the ball
                    jump
run
                                        aim
          catch the ball

net   *net*
      the centre circle
                              the semi-circle

          A netball court

You have to throw the ball into the net to score.

Football ———————————————— page 14

What do you need to play football?

                              a pair of shorts
a shirt   a whistle
Advantage to Wales!   a football

a referee   boots

                    The Welsh
                    football team.
                    There are eleven
                    in the team.

Football ———————————————— page 15

When playing football you have to...

kick   pass   head
          attack
defend
                              goal

              the centre circle
                        the touch line
                    the penalty box
score

                    A football pitch
          You have to kick the ball into the goal
                    to score.

Where is the ball? ———————————————— page 16

                    The snooker ball is in the pocket.
The rugby ball is between the posts.
                    The cricket ball is over the boundary.
The tennis ball is over the net.
                    The football is in the goal.
The netball is in the net.

3

Byd y Bêl

Rhagarweiniad

Nod y llyfr hwn yw cyflwyno geirfa a phatrymau sylfaenol ar gyfer nifer o gêmau cyfarwydd. Cyn darllen y llyfr, dylai'r disgyblion fod yn gyfarwydd â'r patrymau iaith canlynol:

Beth sy ar ...?
Ble mae'r ...?
Pwy sy'n ...?
Beth sy eisiau i ...?
Sut mae ...?
Beth mae'r bachgen yn wneud?
Sawl ...?
Pa liw yw ...?
Wyt ti'n gallu ...?
Oes ... gyda ti?

Cyflwyno'r llyfr

Yn ogystal â darllen y llyfr fel dosbarth gyda'r athro/athrawes/y disgyblion ar eu pennau eu hunain, gellir defnyddio taflunydd dros ysgwydd i gyflwyno'r wybodaeth. Wrth wneud hyn, gellir holi'r disgyblion am yr hyn sydd ar y dudalen e.e.

Beth sy ar dudalen 10?
Beth sy eisiau i chwarae criced?
Pa liw yw crys Cymru?
Pwy sy'n taclo?

Dyma syniadau ar gyfer gweithgareddau yn seiliedig ar Daflen 1 a 2 ar dudalennau 7 ac 8 y Llawlyfr hwn.

Gweithgareddau yn seiliedig ar Daflen 1

Darllen a dweud
I baratoi ar gyfer y gweithgareddau hyn bydd angen llungopïo Taflen 1 a'i thorri i greu set o 12 o gardiau llun a gair.
Y bwriad yw cysylltu offer gêmau â'r man lle y chwaraeir y gêm. Bydd y plant yn darllen yr eirfa ar y cardiau wrth chwarae.

• Gêm i un plentyn:
Taenu'r cardiau wyneb i fyny a chwilio am barau.
(1) Darllen a dweud: "pêl rygbi ... cae rygbi ... pâr" nes paru'r cardiau i gyd.
(2) Fel uchod ond darllen a dweud
"Mae pêl rygbi gyda fi (*neu* Mae pêl rygbi gen i.)
Mae cae rygbi gyda fi.
Mae pâr gyda fi."

Introduction

The aim of this book is to introduce basic vocabulary and patterns for a number of familiar games. Before reading the book, pupils should be familiar with the following language patterns:

Beth sy ar ...?
Ble mae'r ...?
Pwy sy'n ...?
Beth sy eisiau i ...?
Sut mae ...?
Beth mae'r bachgen yn wneud?
Sawl ...?
Pa liw yw ...?
Wyt ti'n gallu ...?
Oes ... gyda ti?

Presenting the book

As well as reading the book as a class with the teacher/the pupils by themselves, an overhead projector can be used to convey the information. While doing this, you can question the pupils on the content of the pages e.g.

Beth sy ar dudalen 10?
Beth sy eisiau i chwarae criced?
Pa liw yw crys Cymru?
Pwy sy'n taclo?

Here are some ideas for activities based on Taflen 1 a 2 on pages 7 and 8 of this Guide.

Activities based on Taflen 1

Reading and speaking
To prepare for these activities you will need to photocopy Taflen 1 and cut it to produce a set of 12 picture and word cards.
The aim is to match a game's equipment with the place where the game is played. The children will read the vocabulary on the cards as they play.

• A game for one child:
Spread the cards face up and look for pairs.
(1) Read and say: "pêl rygbi ... cae rygbi ... pâr" until all the cards have been paired.
(2) As above but read and say
"Mae pêl rygbi gyda fi (*or* Mae pêl rygbi gen i.)
Mae cae rygbi gyda fi.
Mae pâr gyda fi."

- Gêm i ddau blentyn:

Bydd angen cadw cardiau'r offer a chardiau'r mannau chwarae ar wahân neu eu llungopïo ar bapur o liw gwahanol.

Taenu'r cardiau wyneb i waered.
Bydd y plant yn cymryd eu tro i godi un cerdyn o grŵp yr offer ac un o grŵp y mannau chwarae ac yn darllen a dweud beth sydd arnynt, e.e.
1) "bwrdd snwcer ... peli a ciw snwcer ... pâr!" *neu* "bwrdd snwcer ... pêl rygbi ... dim pâr."
2) Fel uchod, bydd y plant yn cymryd eu tro i godi un cerdyn o grŵp yr offer ac un o grŵp y mannau chwarae ond yn darllen a dweud, e.e. "Mae bwrdd snwcer gyda fi ... Mae peli a ciw snwcer gyda fi ... Mae pâr gyda fi!" *neu* "Mae bwrdd snwcer gyda fi ... Mae cae pêl-droed gyda fi ... Does dim pâr gyda fi."
3) Codi un cerdyn o grŵp yr offer ac un o grŵp y mannau chwarae, ac os ydynt yn cyd-fynd, bydd y plentyn yn dweud, e.e. "Mae pêl-droed gyda fi ... Mae cae pêl-droed gyda fi ... Rwy'n gallu chwarae pêl-droed."

Cofio a dweud
I baratoi ar gyfer y gweithgareddau hyn bydd angen llungopïo Taflen 1 a'i thorri i greu set o 24 o gardiau, sef 12 o gardiau llun a 12 o gardiau gair (drwy dorri'r cardiau gwreiddiol ar hyd y llinellau rhwng y geiriau a'r lluniau).

Y bwriad yw darllen ac adnabod ystyr geiriau.

- Gêm i un plentyn:
Taenu'r cardiau wyneb i fyny.
Bydd y plentyn yn dewis cerdyn gair ac yn darllen e.e. "pêl-rwyd", yna'n dewis cerdyn llun (pêl-rwyd) i gyfateb a'u gosod wrth ymyl ei gilydd.
Fel uchod, ond ychwanegu: "Rwy'n hoffi pêl-rwyd" *neu* "Dw i ddim yn hoffi pêl-rwyd."

- Gêm i ddau blentyn:

Bydd angen cadw cardiau'r lluniau a chardiau'r geiriau ar wahân.
Taenu'r cardiau wyneb i waered.
Bydd y plant yn cymryd eu tro i droi drosodd ddau gerdyn, un â llun ac un â gair, a dweud:
"pêl-droed (llun) ... pêl-droed (gair) ... Mae pâr gyda fi!" *neu* "pêl-droed (llun) ... cwrt tennis (gair) ... Does dim pâr gyda fi."

- A game for two children:

The equipment cards and the playing area cards will need to be kept apart or photocopied on different coloured paper.

Spread the cards face down.
The children will take turns to pick up one card each from the equipment group and the playing area group and read and say what is on them, e.g.
1) "bwrdd snwcer ... peli a ciw snwcer ... pâr!" *or* "bwrdd snwcer ... pêl rygbi ... dim pâr."
2) As above, the children will take turns to pick up one card each from the equipment group and the playing area group but will read and say, e.g. "Mae bwrdd snwcer gyda fi ... Mae peli a ciw snwcer gyda fi ... Mae pâr gyda fi!" *or* "Mae bwrdd snwcer gyda fi ... Mae cae pêl-droed gyda fi ... Does dim pâr gyda fi."
3) Pick up one card each from the equipment group and the playing area group, and if they match, the child will say, e.g. "Mae pêl-droed gyda fi ... Mae cae pêl-droed gyda fi ... Rwy'n gallu chwarae pêl-droed."

Remembering and saying
To prepare for these activities you will need to photocopy Taflen 1 and cut it to produce a set of 24 cards, that is 12 picture cards and 12 word cards (by cutting the original cards along the lines between the words and pictures).

The aim is to read and recognise the meaning of words.

- A game for one child:
Spread the cards face up. The child will choose a word card and read e.g. "pêl-rwyd", and will then choose a picture card (pêl-rwyd) to match and place them next to each other.
As above, but adding: "Rwy'n hoffi pêl-rwyd" *or* "Dw i ddim yn hoffi pêl-rwyd."

- A game for two children:

The picture cards and the word cards will need to be kept apart.
Spread the cards face down. The children will take turns to turn over two cards, one with a picture and one with a word, and say:
"pêl-droed (picture) ... pêl-droed (word) ... Mae pâr gyda fi!" *or* "pêl-droed (picture) ... cwrt tennis (word) ... Does dim pâr gyda fi."

Gweithgareddau yn seiliedig ar Daflen 2

Darllen, deall a gwneud

I baratoi ar gyfer y gweithgareddau hyn bydd angen llungopïo Taflen 2 a'i thorri i greu set o 8 o gardiau llun a gair.

- Gêm i bâr neu grŵp:

Bydd un plentyn yn darllen yn uchel yr hyn sydd ar un o'r cardiau â berfau trin pêl arnynt (heb ddangos y llun i neb).
Os ydy'r partner/grŵp yn deall byddant yn meimio'r symudiad.

- Gêm ddosbarth:

Bydd un plentyn o flaen y dosbarth yn dewis un o'r cardiau â berfau trin pêl arnynt ac yn meimio'r symudiad. Bydd y plant eraill yn dyfalu beth mae e'n ei wneud ac yn dweud y geiriau.

- Gêm ddosbarth:

Bydd yr athro/athrawes yn gofyn "Pwy sy'n gallu taflu'r bêl? Dangoswch i fi." Bydd y plant yn ymateb drwy feimio'r symudiad, neu drwy arddangos y symudiad gyda phêl go iawn.

- Gêm ddosbarth:

Dysgu'r gorchmynion :

daliwch y bêl   *bownsiwch y bêl*
taflwch y bêl   *bwrwch y bêl*
pasiwch y bêl   *potiwch y bêl*
peniwch y bêl   *ciciwch y bêl*

a chwarae "Mae Seimon yn dweud" gan ddefnyddio'r gorchmynion uchod yn unig.

Gellir hefyd chwarae gêmau cyfateb llun a gair gyda'r lluniau/geiriau ar Daflen 2 drwy wneud copi ychwanegol o'r cardiau a thorri ar y llinellau rhwng y geiriau a'r lluniau. (Mae manylion sut i chwarae yng nghyfarwyddiadau gêmau Taflen 1).

Activities based on Taflen 2

Reading, understanding and doing

To prepare for these activities you will need to photocopy Taflen 2 and cut it to produce a set of 8 picture and word cards.

- A game for a pair or group:

One child will read aloud what is on one of the cards with ball handling verbs (without showing the picture to anyone).
If the partner/group understands they will mime the movement.

- A class game:

One child in front of the class will choose one of the cards with ball handling verbs and mime the movement. The other children will guess what he is doing and say the words.

- A class game:

The teacher will ask: "Pwy sy'n gallu taflu'r bêl? Dangoswch i fi." The children will respond by miming the movement, or by showing the movement with a real ball.

- A class game:

Learn the commands:

daliwch y bêl   *bownsiwch y bêl*
taflwch y bêl   *bwrwch y bêl*
pasiwch y bêl   *potiwch y bêl*
peniwch y bêl   *ciciwch y bêl*

and play "Simon says" using the above commands only.

You can also play games matching pictures and words with the pictures/words on Taflen 2 by making an additional copy of the cards and cutting on the lines between the words and pictures. (Details of how to play can be found in the instructions for games for Taflen 1).

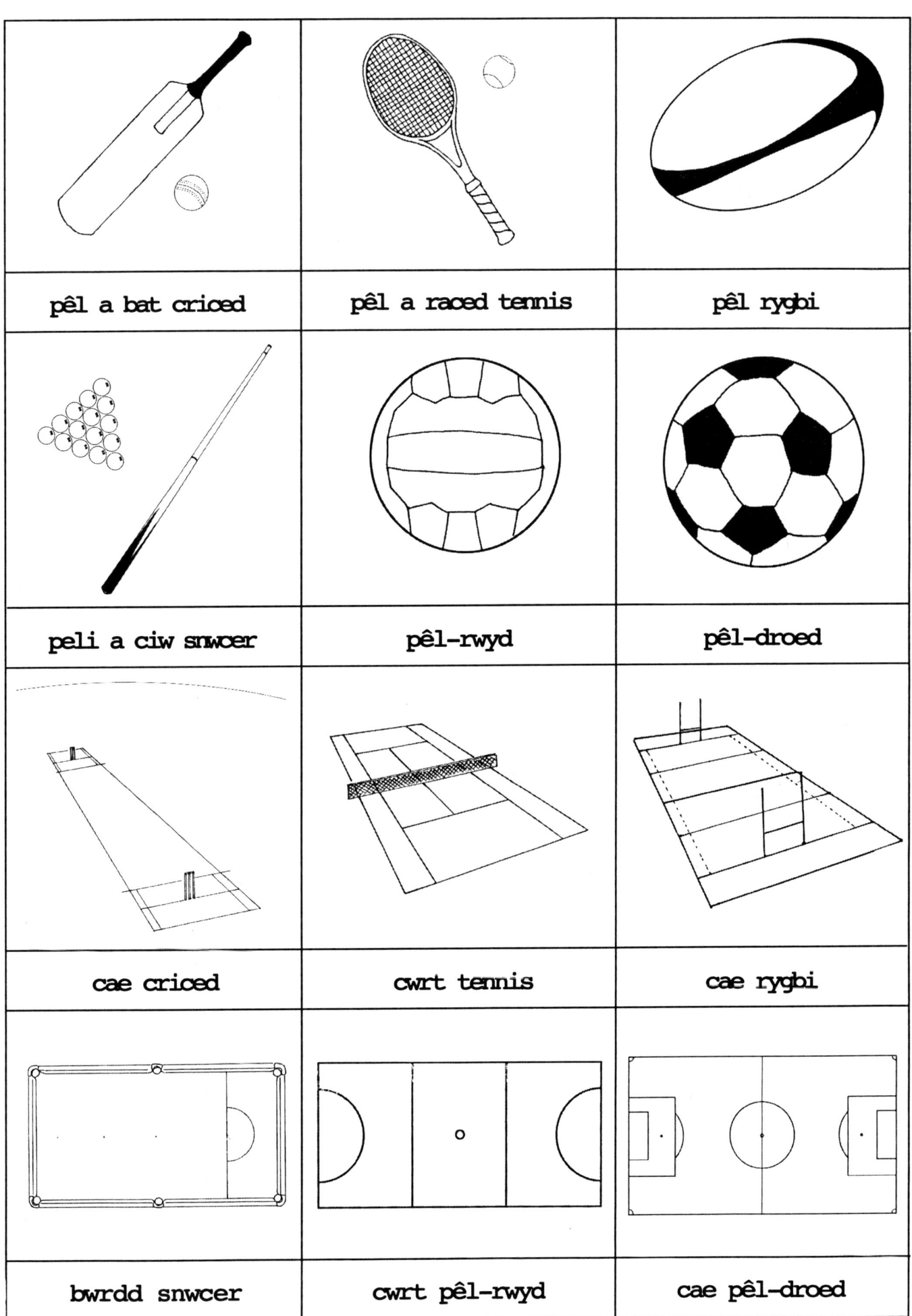

pêl a bat criced	pêl a raced tennis	pêl rygbi
peli a ciw snwcer	pêl-rwyd	pêl-droed
cae criced	cwrt tennis	cae rygbi
bwrdd snwcer	cwrt pêl-rwyd	cae pêl-droed

dal y bêl	bowsio'r bêl
taflu'r bêl	bwrw'r bêl
pasio'r bêl	potio'r bêl
penio'r bêl	cicio'r bêl

Do you like skiing and swimming?
Do you enjoy driving a motor bike and riding?
Are you mad on rollerblading?

Come to the Urdd Camp, at Llangrannog!

Do you like canoeing and going on an adventure course?
Do you enjoy tenpin bowling and climbing?
Are you mad on swimming?

Come to the Urdd camp, at Glan-llyn!

*Come and have fun
And a good time with us!*

Children and young people enjoy a holiday at the Urdd camp.

What is the Urdd?

The Urdd, Urdd Gobaith Cymru, is a movement for children and young people under 25 years of age.

The Urdd is fun – all kinds of sports, competitions in the Eisteddfod ... and of course, brilliant holidays.

There's a fantastic swimming pool at Llangrannog.

There's a brilliant swimming pool at Glan-llyn too.

This is the swimming pool. Before going into the swimming pool, you have to walk through the foot bath. The water is cold in the foot bath. But the water is warm in the swimming pool. The water is 31° C.

There is a lifeguard looking after the children. He watches the boys and girls in the swimming pool. "These are the rules," he says. "No running. No pushing. No jumping into the water."

No running!

lifeguard

The children enjoy swimming. Sometimes they play water polo.

Where is Llangrannog?

Llangrannog is by the seaside.
Llangrannog is between Aberystwyth and Cardigan.

Where is Glan-llyn?

Glan-llyn is near Bala.
Glan-llyn is by Bala Lake.

What is there at Llangrannog? There is an adventure course at Llangrannog.

There is an adventure course at Glan-llyn too.

This is the adventure course. There is bark on the ground. You have to wear a helmet, long trousers and a long-sleeved jumper on the adventure course.

The children are walking across a rope bridge. They are holding tight onto both ropes.

The children work in groups on the adventure course.

rope bridge

We've got a rollerblading hall at Llangrannog. Is there a rollerblading hall at Glan-llyn?

Yes, there's a rollerblading hall at Glan-llyn too.

Here are the children in the rollerblading hall. They are wearing special shoes, rollerblading shoes. There are little wheels under the shoes. They also have to wear wristbands.

To avoid an accident, all the children rollerblade straight ahead.

"With the music - one, two, three, away we go!"

wheels   wristbands

Put your rollerblading shoes back on the shelf

The children enjoy rollerblading to the disco music.
Rollerblading is brilliant.

page 9

*There's a big sports hall at Glan-llyn.
Is there a sports hall at Llangrannog?*

Yes, there's a sports hall at Llangrannog too.

Here are the children in the sports hall. You have to wear trainers in the sports hall. The children are playing games.

After using the equipment, you have to tidy the hall. The equipment must be kept tidy in the storeroom.

page 10

*There are horses at Llangrannog.
The children can ride at the camp.*

This is the Big Barn. The boys and girls are wearing special hats. You have to wear a hard hat to ride a horse.

hard hat   bridle

The children are learning how to ride.

After learning how to ride, the children go for a ride on the horses. There is a special track around the camp.
They work in groups of two. One child walks on the left in front of the horse. The other child is on the horse's back.

page 11

At Glan-llyn, the children can canoe.

Here are the canoes on the lake. You have to wear a lifejacket and a helmet to go in a canoe. The children use a paddle to move through the water.

Before going on the lake, the children learn how to come out of the canoe in an accident. There is a rescue boat on the lake too. The rescue boat helps the children in an accident.

page 12

At Llangrannog, the children enjoy driving motor bikes.

This is the motor bike track. To go on the bikes, the children wear helmets. You have to wear long trousers and a long-sleeved jumper too. You have to drive the bikes on the track.

old tyres

There are 50cc and 80cc bikes at Llangrannog. The bikes go quickly round the track. The children enjoy driving the bikes quickly.

page 13

There aren't any motor bikes at Glan-llyn. But there is tenpin bowling here.

This is the tenpin bowling centre. There are four long alleys in the hall. At the bottom of each alley, there are ten skittles. You have to hit the ten skittles with the big ball. The ball is heavy.

Each player is allowed to roll the ball twice.

page 14

There's no tenpin bowling at Llangrannog. But there is a ski slope here.

This is the ski slope. The children are wearing long trousers, a long-sleeved jumper and gloves. You have to wear gloves on the slope. The children are learning how to ski.

After learning to ski, the children go on the lift up the slope. They ski down the ski slope. The slope is very slippery because there is water on the slope.

There are a 100 metres from the top of the ski slope to the bottom.

There isn't a ski slope at Glan-llyn. But there is a climbing wall here.

This is the climbing wall. You have to wear a helmet and a harness to climb the wall.

The instructor stands at the bottom. He watches the climber closely.

The harness keeps the climber safe.

There are lots of other things to do at Llangrannog and Glan-llyn.

Here are some of them:
Llangrannog
- tobogganing
- parachute games
- swimming in the sea

Glan-llyn
- sailing
- white water rafting
- sleeping on the bivi
- building a raft

There is more information about the Urdd camps on:
- the Urdd video, available from Swyddfa'r Urdd, Ffordd Llanbadarn, Aberystwyth SY23 1EY
  Tel: 01970 613100
- the Urdd website, www.urdd.org
- Urdd Gobaith Cymru 75: CD-ROM y Dathlu, available from Swyddfa'r Urdd

Hwyl y Gwersyll

Rhagarweiniad

Nod y llyfr hwn yw cyflwyno gwybodaeth am wersylloedd yr Urdd yng Nglan-llyn a Llangrannog a rhoi blas i'r darllenwyr o'r gweithgareddau a geir yno.

Cyn darllen y llyfr, dylai'r disgyblion fod yn gyfarwydd â'r patrymau iaith canlynol:

Ydych chi'n hoffi / mwynhau / dwli ar ....?
Ble mae ...?
Beth ydy ...?
Oes ...?
Ydy ...?　　a'r atebion perthnasol.

Ceir nifer o frawddegau sy'n cynnwys **rhaid** yn y llyfr.

Cyflwyno'r llyfr

Yn ogystal â darllen y llyfr fel dosbarth gyda'r athro/athrawes/y disgyblion ar eu pennau eu hunain, gellir defnyddio taflunydd dros ysgwydd i gyflwyno'r wybodaeth. Wrth wneud hyn, gellir holi'r disgyblion am yr hyn sydd ar y dudalen e.e.
Beth mae'r plant yn wneud yma?
Beth mae'r plant yn wisgo?
Wyt ti'n hoffi/mwynhau llafnrolio?
Oes pwll nofio yn Llangrannog?
Wyt ti'n gallu sgio?
Oes pont o raffau yn y cwrs antur?

Taflen Waith 1
Gellir defnyddio'r lluniau sydd ar y daflen hon fel cardiau fflach. Drwy chwyddo maint y lluniau, mae'n bosibl eu defnyddio fel cymorth i gyflwyno geirfa rhai o'r gweithgareddau llai cyfarwydd.

Gellir defnyddio'r daflen mewn tair ffordd:

• cysylltu llun â gair drwy dynnu llinellau i gysylltu'r lluniau â'r geiriau/ymadroddion sy'n eu disgrifio (wrth lungopïo, dylid gorchuddio'r rhestr sydd ar waelod y daflen)

• dewis y gair/ymadrodd sy'n cyd-fynd â phob llun o'r rhestr ar waelod y daflen ac ysgrifennu'r geiriau/ymadroddion hynny dan y lluniau fel labeli (wrth lungopïo, dylid gorchuddio'r geiriau sydd gyferbyn â'r lluniau)

Introduction

The aim of this book is to provide information about the Urdd camps at Glan-llyn and Llangrannog and give readers a flavour of the activities available there.

Before reading the book, pupils should be familiar with the following language patterns:

Ydych chi'n hoffi / mwynhau / dwli ar ...?
Ble mae ...?
Beth ydy ...?
Oes ...?
Ydy ...?　　and the relevant answers.

A number of sentences containing **rhaid** are used in the book.

Presenting the book

As well as reading the book as a class with the teacher/the pupils by themselves, an overhead projector can be used to convey the information. While doing this, you can question the pupils on the content of the pages, e.g.
Beth mae'r plant yn wneud yma?
Beth mae'r plant yn wisgo?
Wyt ti'n hoffi/mwynhau llafnrolio?
Oes pwll nofio yn Llangrannog?
Wyt ti'n gallu sgio?
Oes pont o raffau yn y cwrs antur?

Taflen Waith 1
The pictures on this worksheet can be used as flash cards. By enlarging the pictures, they can be used as an aid to introduce the vocabulary of some of the activities which are less familiar.

This sheet can be used in three ways;

• linking a picture with a word by drawing lines to connect the pictures with the words/phrases that describe them (when photocopying, the list at the bottom of the sheet should be covered)

• choosing the word/phrase that corresponds to each picture from the list at the bottom of the sheet and writing those words/phrases under the pictures as labels (when photocopying, the words opposite the pictures should be covered)

- labelu'r lluniau heb help (wrth lungopïo, dylid gorchuddio'r ddwy restr).

Taflen Waith 2

Nod y daflen hon yw helpu disgyblion i ymgyfarwyddo â phatrwm iaith arbennig a chadarnhau geirfa'r gweithgareddau ar yr un pryd.

e.e. **Wyt ti'n hoffi/mwynhau …?**
Ydw/Nac ydw
Ga i …? Cei/Na chei
Est ti i …? Do/Naddo

Gêm i ddau yw hon. Dylid rhoi copi o Daflen Waith 2 i'r ddau bartner yn ogystal â thri chownter yr un i'w rhoi ar y lluniau sydd wedi eu dyfalu'n gywir. Cyn dechrau chwarae, dylai pob plentyn ddewis tri gweithgaredd a'u hysgrifennu ar ddarn o bapur. Rhaid defnyddio'r patrwm sy'n cael ei ymarfer i ddarganfod pa weithgareddau a ddewiswyd. Y cyntaf i ddyfalu'r tri gweithgaredd sy'n ennill.

Ar ddiwedd y gêm, gall y ddau bartner/enillydd fynd at yr athro/athrawes a dweud wrtho/wrthi am y gweithgareddau a ddewiswyd.
e.e Dw i'n hoffi/mwynhau canŵio. Es i i nofio.

Taflen Waith 3

Nod y daflen waith hon yw annog y disgyblion i ysgrifennu am brofiad dychmygol neu brofiad go iawn os ydyn nhw wedi ymweld â Gwersylloedd yr Urdd.

Cyn defnyddio'r daflen waith hon, dylid sicrhau bod y disgyblion yn gyfarwydd â chynnwys y llyfr a'u bod yn gyfarwydd â thrafod y gweithgareddau gyda'r athro/athrawes/ymhlith ei gilydd.

Er mai ymadrodd yn hytrach na brawddeg a roddir yn yr enghraifft ar y daflen waith, gellir gofyn am frawddeg i roi 'barn' am y gweithgaredd.

e.e. Cyrraedd … – Dw i'n hoffi …
Chwarac gêmau – Dw i'n dwli ar chwarae gêmau.

Gellir gofyn i'r disgyblion ysgrifennu cardiau post hefyd fel sail i'w hysgrifennu.

Gellir defnyddio'r wybodaeth yn y dyddiadur hefyd i greu poster/taflen hysbysebu ar gyfer y gwersylloedd.
e.e. Dewch i Lan-llyn! Dewch i fwynhau …

- labelling the pictures without any help (when photocopying, both lists should be covered).

Taflen Waith 2

The aim of this worksheet is to help pupils become familiar with a particular language pattern and consolidate vocabulary at the same time.

e.g. **Wyt ti'n hoffi/mwynhau …?**
Ydw/Nac ydw
Ga i …? Cei/Na chei
Est ti i …? Do/Naddo

This is a game for two. A copy of Taflen Waith 2 should be given to both partners as well as three counters to be placed on the pictures that have been guessed correctly. Before starting to play, each child should choose three activities and write them on a piece of paper. The pattern being practised must be used to discover which activities have been chosen. The first to guess the three activities is the winner.

At the end of the game, the two partners/winner can go to the teacher and tell him/her about the activities chosen.
e.g. Dw i'n hoffi/mwynhau canŵio. Es i i nofio.

Taflen Waith 3

The aim of this worksheet is to encourage pupils to write about an imaginary experience or a real experience if they have visited the Urdd camps.

Before using this worksheet, you should ensure that the pupils are familiar with the content of the book and that they are familiar with discussing the activities with the teacher/amongst themselves.

Even though the example on the worksheet gives an expression not a sentence, it is possible to ask for a sentence to give an 'opinion' of the activity.

e.g. Cyrraedd … – Dw i'n hoffi …
Chwarae gêmau – Dw i'n dwli ar chwarae gêmau.

You can also ask the pupils to write postcards as a basis for their writing.

The information in the diary can also be used to create a poster/advertising leaflet for the camps.
e.g. Dewch i Lan-llyn! Dewch i fwynhau …

bowlio deg

. . . .

. . . .

llafnrolio

marchogaeth

chwarae gêmau

. . . .

. . . .

gyrru beiciau modur

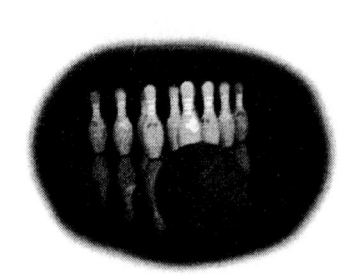

nofio

. . . .

dringo

sgio

. . . .

mynd ar y cwrs antur

. . . .

. . . .

canŵio

. . . .

. . . .

bowlio deg	sgio	mynd ar gefn ceffyl	llafnrolio
dringo	mynd ar y cwrs antur	chwarae gêmau	canŵio nofio
			mynd ar y beiciau modur

14

Dewiswch dri gweithgaredd o'r rhai sy ar y daflen. Rhaid i chi ofyn cwestiynau i'ch partner i gael gwybod pa weithgareddau mae e neu hi wedi dewis.

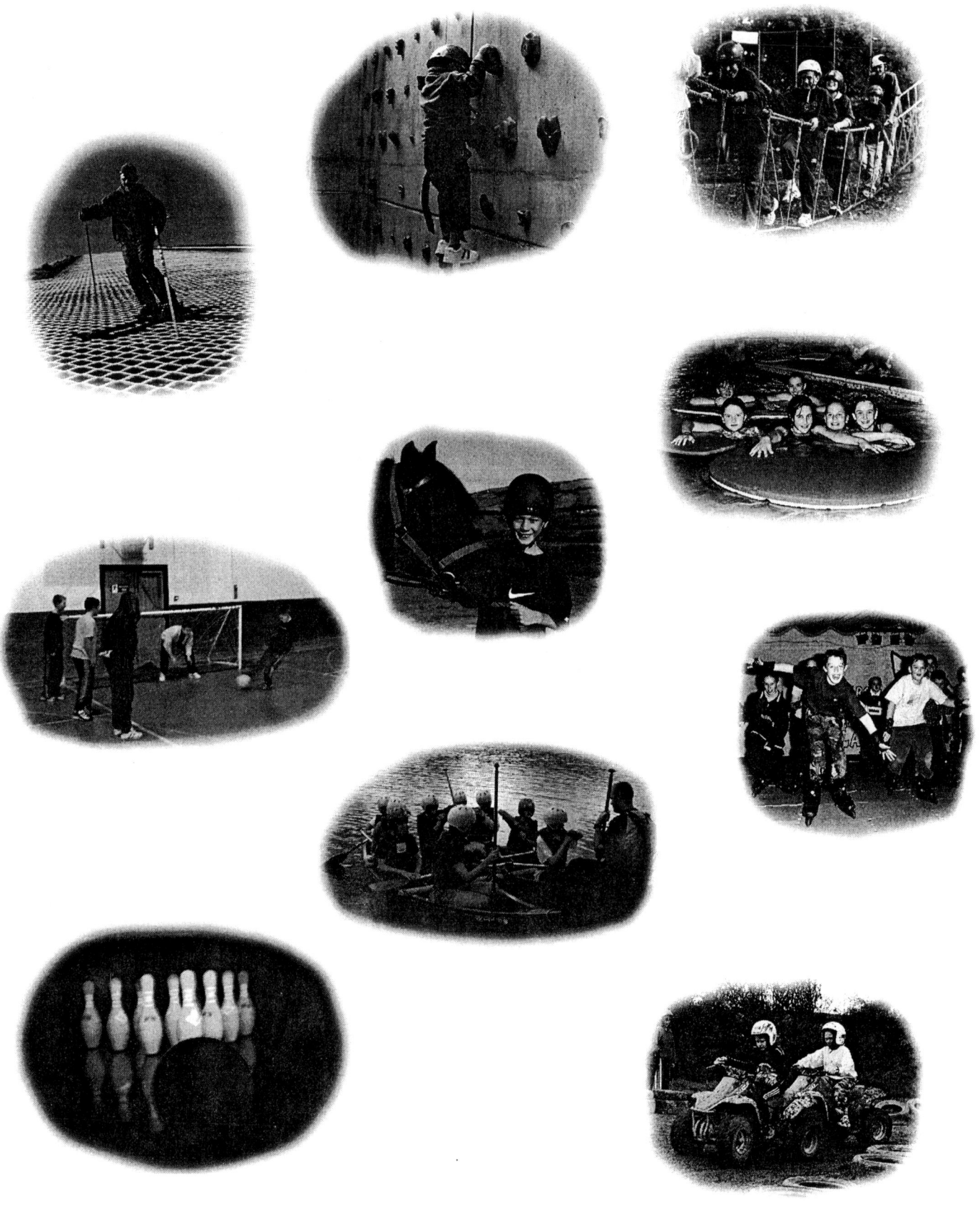

Hwyl y Gwersyll   **Taflen Waith 3**

Rydych chi'n mynd ar wyliau i Wersyll yr Urdd o ddydd Llun i ddydd Gwener. Rhaid i chi wneud 2 weithgaredd bob dydd. Dydych chi ddim yn gallu gwneud yr un gweithgaredd fwy nag unwaith. Ysgrifennwch yn eich dyddiadur yn dweud beth wnaethoch chi bob dydd.

Bore dydd Llun: Cyrraedd Llangrannog

_____

Prynhawn dydd Llun: ....
_____

Bore dydd Mawrth: ....
_____

Prynhawn dydd Mawrth: ....
_____

Bore dydd Mercher: ....
_____

Prynhawn dydd Mercher: ....
_____

Bore dydd Iau: ....
_____

Prynhawn dydd Iau: ....
_____

Bore dydd Gwener: ....
_____

Prynhawn dydd Gwener: Mynd adref
_____

Many people enjoy going on a skiing holiday. But there isn't enough snow in Britain, apart from Scotland. So, many people go abroad to ski.

France, Austria, Switzerland, Italy and Andorra are popular places. There is plenty of snow there!

You can ski somewhere all year round. During our winter, people ski in Europe and North America, that is, in the northern hemisphere.

When it is summer in Wales, you can ski in New Zealand, Australia, Chile or Argentina. All these countries are in the southern hemisphere.

You have to practise before going to ski in a foreign country.

There are dry slopes in several places in our country. You can have skiing lessons on a dry ski slope.

Here are some of the dry slopes in Wales.

But there is no real snow there.

You have to go to a snow dome to get real snow. There is one in Tamworth in the Birmingham area. The indoor skiing slope there was the first, with real snow, in Europe.

You can ski on real snow in the dome throughout the year!

You can have a lot of fun sledging there too.

You have to have suitable clothes and equipment for skiing.

You need:
ski boots
skis
poles
a helmet
a ski suit
gloves
sunglasses

You must also remember to take sunscreen and lip balm.

The snow is cold, so you have to wrap up warm. The clothes must be waterproof too in order to keep dry in the snow.
You need sunglasses, sunscreen and lip balm too because the snow makes the sun more dazzling.

The next step is to learn to ski. The children in this picture are beginning to learn to ski on snow. They are having lessons in a group and are having fun learning together.

Balance is very important when skiing.

You have to bend your legs a little in order to keep your balance.

You can ski downhill and on level ground. In the Alps, people ski downhill usually because there are many mountains there.

Skiing on level ground – cross-country skiing – is very popular in countries that get a lot of snow, like the Scandinavian countries.

People started skiing in Scandinavia thousands of years ago. Skiing was a good way of travelling on the snow in winter.

People who ski well can take part in competitions. Many of these competitions are races.

There are many skiing races in the Winter Olympic Games. One competition is downhill skiing.

The skiers ski down the slope as fast as possible. They ski down one after the other. The one who finishes the race in the shortest time is the winner.

The best skiers can go over 100 km per hour!

Another type of race is the slalom race.

In a slalom, the skiers race against the clock, but this time they have to go between the gates on the course. They ski zigzag to the bottom.

The one who reaches the bottom in the shortest time is the winner.

Another event at the Winter Olympic Games is ski jumping. Ski jumping is very exciting.

The skier races down a steep ramp and then jumps high in the air.

In competitions, judges give the skiers marks for each jump. They get marks for how they jump and for the length of the jump too.

Some of the world's best skiers can jump 100 metres.

Acrobatic skiing is another way of skiing. There are three types of acrobatic skiing.

One is doing ballet movements while skiing. The skier dances to music on the snow.

Another type is jumping and turning while skiing on uneven ground.

The third type is to do tricks in the air.

Snowboarding is a way of moving on snow too. It is similar to skateboarding – but on snow.

You have to have a wide board similar to a skateboard. Your two feet are tied onto the board.

Snowboarders can ride on open ground, on mountains or through trees. They can do all kinds of tricks in the air too.

You can learn to snowboard on a dry ski slope.

Snowboarders can take part in competitions too.

Sometimes, they jump and do tricks in the air. Judges give marks for each performance.

Snowboarders race too. There are slalom races, similar to skiing races, in the Winter Olympic Games.

Snowboarders can turn corners very well because the board is short. They can move almost as fast as skiers on a slalom course!

Llethrau Llithrig!

Rhagarweiniad

Pwrpas y llyfr hwn yw cyflwyno gwybodaeth am sgio, o lefel gwyliau i'r Chwaraeon Olympaidd.

Cyn darllen a thrafod y testun, dylid sicrhau bod y disgyblion yn gyfarwydd â'r patrymau iaith canlynol:
Mae'n bosib ...
Rhaid ...
Mae digon o ...
Does dim ...
Yr un sy'n ...

Cyflwyno'r llyfr

Yn ogystal â darllen y llyfr fel dosbarth gyda'r athro/athrawes/y disgyblion ar eu pennau eu hunain, gellir defnyddio taflunydd dros ysgwydd i gyflwyno'r wybodaeth. Wrth wneud hynny, gellir holi'r disgyblion am yr hyn sydd ar y tudalennau e.e.
Beth sy ar y posteri ar dudalen 3?
Ble mae llethrau sgio sych yng Nghymru?
Sut ddillad sy eisiau i sgio?
Ble gallwch chi sgio ym mis Awst?
Oes eira iawn ar lethr sgio sych?

Ymgyfarwyddo â'r eirfa

Gweithgareddau posibl:

a)   Disgrifio lluniau/darluniadau unigol. Holi beth sy'n digwydd mewn llun.

b)   Darllen a thrafod cynnwys mapiau, posteri, rhestrau a diagramau.

c) Defnyddio'r mynegai.
Gofyn i'r plant edrych yn y mynegai i gael ateb i gwestiynau tebyg i:
Beth sy yn Tamworth?
Beth sy eisiau i eirfyrddio?

ch) Llunio holiadur
Mewn grwpiau, gofyn i'r plant lunio holiaduron.
e.e. Pwy sy wedi bod yn sgio ar lethr sgio sych/ ar eira, pwy fyddai'n hoffi dysgu sgio, ac yn y blaen.

Introduction

The purpose of this book is to give information on skiing, from a holiday level to the Olympic Games.

Before reading and discussing the text, you should ensure that the pupils are familiar with the following language patterns:
Mae'n bosib ...
Rhaid ...
Mae digon o ...
Does dim ...
Yr un sy'n ...

Presenting the book

As well as reading the book as a class with the teacher/the pupils by themselves, an overhead projector can be used to convey the information. While doing this, you can question the pupils on the content of the pages e.g.
Beth sy ar y posteri ar dudalen 3?
Ble mae llethrau sgio sych yng Nghymru?
Sut ddillad sy eisiau i sgio?
Ble gallwch chi sgio ym mis Awst?
Oes eira iawn ar lethr sgio sych?

Getting used to the vocabulary

Possible activities:

a)   Describing individual pictures/illustrations. Asking what is happening in a picture.

b)   Reading and discussing the content of maps, posters, lists and diagrams.

c)   Using the index.
Asking the children to look in the index to find the answer to questions like:
Beth sy yn Tamworth?
Beth sy eisiau i eirfyrddio?

ch) Designing a questionnaire
In groups, ask the children to design questionnaires.
e.g. Who has been skiing on a dry ski slope/on snow, who would like to learn to ski, etc.

Y grwpiau eraill i lenwi'r holiaduron.

d) Cartŵn
Llunio cyfres o luniau cartŵn gyda swigod yn hysbysebu gwyliau sgio.

dd) Cynnal cwis. Rhannu'r dosbarth yn grwpiau a gofyn i bob grŵp osod chwe chwestiwn sydd ag atebion clir yn y llyfr. Cynnal cwis rhwng y grwpiau h.y. pob grŵp i geisio ateb cwestiynau'r grwpiau eraill.

Trefnu gwers sgio

Gellir gofyn i'r plant weithio gyda phartner i greu sgwrs lle mae un yn gofyn i'r llall, neu'n ei ffonio, i ofyn a fyddai'n hoffi mynd i gael gwers sgio neu eirfyrddio gydag e/hi ar lethr sgio sych. Bydd angen iddynt drafod y lleoliad, yr amser, sut maen nhw'n mynd yno ac yn y blaen.

Trefnu gwyliau sgio

Gellir gofyn i'r plant ddychmygu bod yr ysgol neu glwb y maent yn perthyn iddo yn bwriadu trefnu gwyliau sgio a bod gofyn iddynt hwy helpu gyda'r trefniadau. Bydd angen iddynt benderfynu ar leoliad, trefnu dyddiadau, manylion teithio, y paratoadau, pa ddillad/offer fydd eu hangen ac yn y blaen. Dyma rai gweithgareddau posibl:

i) Creu poster i hysbysebu'r gwyliau.

ii) Llunio amserlen o'r hyn fydd yn digwydd i baratoi ar gyfer y gwyliau ac yn ystod y gwyliau ei hun.

iii) Ysgrifennu llythyr at rieni plant yr ysgol/clwb yn rhoi manylion y daith, disgrifio'r lleoliad, sôn am y paratoadau ac yn y blaen.

iv) Dychmygu eu bod wedi mynd ar y gwyliau sgio uchod ac ysgrifennu cerdyn post i'w anfon at eu rhieni.

v) Ysgrifennu adroddiad dychmygol yn sôn am yr hyn a wnaethant pan oeddent ar y gwyliau uchod.

Gwaith Pellach

Dewis un wlad ble mae'n bosibl sgio.
Gwneud prosiect yn seiliedig ar y wlad honno.

The other groups to fill in the questionnaires.

d) Cartoon
Producing a series of cartoon pictures with speech bubbles to advertise a skiing holiday.

dd) Holding a quiz. Divide the class into groups and ask each group to set six questions which have clear answers in the book. Hold a quiz between the groups i.e. each group to try and answer the other groups' questions.

Arranging a skiing lesson

You could ask the children to work with a partner to create a conversation where one asks or phones the other to ask whether he/she would like to have a skiing or a snowboarding lesson with him/her on a dry ski slope. They will need to discuss the location, the time, how they will get there etc.

Arranging a skiing holiday

You could ask the children to imagine that the school or a club they belong to is arranging a skiing holiday and that they are required to help with the arrangements. They will need to decide on a location, arrange the dates, the travel details, the preparations, what clothes/equipment will be needed etc. Here are some possible activities:

i) Creating a poster to advertise the holiday.

ii) Formulating a timetable of what will happen to prepare for the holiday and during the holiday itself.

iii) Writing a letter to the parents of the children in the school/club giving details of the journey, describing the location, mentioning the preparations etc.

iv) Imagining that they have gone on the above skiing holiday and writing a postcard to send to their parents.

v) Writing an imaginary report on what they did on the skiing holiday mentioned above.

Further Work

Select one country where it is possible to ski.
Do a project based on that country.